THE GIRL IS SMILING

CHERYL MOSKOWITZ was born in 1959 in Chicago, Illinois, moving to the UK in 1970. She studied Psychology at Sussex University, Dramatherapy at Herts College of Art and Design, and Psychodynamic Counselling at Highgate Counselling Centre.

She began writing and performing poetry in the 80's with the poetry collectives Angels of Fire and LIP. In 1996 she co-founded the organisation LAPIDUS (Association for Literary Arts and Personal Development) and taught on the Creative Writing and Personal Development MA at Sussex University from its inception in 1996 until 2010.

In 1998 her first novel *Wyoming Trail* was published by Granta. Her collection of poetry for children *Can it be about me?* illustrated by Ros Asquith is published in 2012 by Janetta Otter-Barry Books (Frances Lincoln Publishers).

She works as a freelance facilitator of creative writing projects in the community for many arts organisations including the Poetry Society, Create Arts, TEXT Writers in Schools, English Touring Opera and the British Council.

Her poems have received awards in the Bridport Prize poetry competition (2010), the Troubadour International Poetry Prize (2010), and the International Hippocrates Prize for Poetry and Medicine (2011).

She lives in London with her husband, a musician, and they have three children.

Cheryl Moskowitz's website: www.cherylmoskowitz.com

The Girl Is Smiling

Cheryl Moskowitz

Circle Time Press

Copyright © Cheryl Moskowitz 2012

ISBN: 978-0-9564082-1-1

First published in Great Britain 2012
by CIRCLE TIME PRESS
info@circletimepress.co.uk

Set in Garamond Premier Pro
Title set in Biro Script by Ingo Zimmerman

Design & Photography by Alastair Gavin

Printed and bound by CPI Group (UK) Ltd, Croydon, CR0 4YY

LEGAL NOTICE

All rights reserved. Without limiting the rights under copyright reserved above, no part of this publication may be reproduced, stored in or introduced into a retrieval system or transmitted, in any form or by any means (electronic, mechanical, photocopying, recording or otherwise), without the prior permission of both the copyright owner and the above publisher of this book.

Cheryl Moskowitz asserts her moral right under Section 77 of the Copyright, Designs and Patents Act 1988 to be identified as the author of this book.

For A, A, G & M

ACKNOWLEDGMENTS

"Moving the Stag Head to Aunt Irma's" published in *Not Only The Dark,* WordAid anthology in aid of ShelterBox Winter 2012; "Correspondence with the Care Home" - second place Open Category Hippocrates Poetry Prize 2011, published in *The Hippocrates Prize – The Winning and Commended Poems* Top Edge Press 2011; "Ices" published in *The Shuffle Anthology* Autumn 2011; "Wednesday" published in *The Winners* The Bridport Prize 2010; "Lifted" published in *Artemis Poetry Magazine* Issue 3 Nov 2009; "I Left My Heart" published in *Long Poem Magazine* Issue 1 Winter 2008/9;

Special thanks to my dear friends (and excellent poets), Wendy French, Maggie Butt and Leslie McGrath, for being such willing and intelligent critics; for the astute feedback given by everyone in Clink Street, North London Stanza and Mimi Khalvati's poetry workshops; and to the Ragdale Foundation and Vermont Studio Center for granting precious time and space to write. And for being the inspiration for so much of my poetry, I am indebted to all my family, especially my children, Alice, George and Martha, without whom my words would be entirely without song or meaning. Finally, for everything else... Alastair.

CONTENTS

The Definition of Things	9
The Visit	10
Composition	12
Still	13
Conscience	14
Lifted	15
I Left My Heart	16
When I draw my last breath	18
Beginnings	19
Standing Stones	20
A Walk in the Park	22
He Disappeared Into Complete Silence 1947 (Plate 1)	23
About Mothers, by Daughters	25
Pianissimo	26
One for the Heart	27
Senescence	28
Asylum	29
Adrift	30
Infinite Space	31
Mrs White	32
On Seeing a Doe in the Prairie by the Bridge	33
Alice	34
Wednesday	36
Recipe	37
Loneliness	38
Wilson Avenue	40
The Art of Forgetting	41
On Age and Beauty	42
Blighted	43
Leaving	44
Travel Sickness	46
Passerine	47

Bird Box	48
Victory	50
Impossible Beauty	51
I was there to tell stories	52
Sorting the Album	53
driving with alice	54
After Making Love on a Sunday Morning	56
Fruit	57
Moving the Stag Head to Aunt Irma's	58
Ices	60
Word Birth	61
Scientific Autobiography	62
Wait To Be Called	63
Or Not to Be	64
Schizophrenic	65
The Starlet	66
Done	67
Maternal Encounters and Thoughts Arising	68
Correspondence with the Care Home	69
Snapshot	70

The Definition of Things

I have been worrying recently
about the definition of things.

Love, for example, and its absence
and it seems to me that the three phones

I have taken to keeping by my bed at night
are an indication of that,

that there really is no clear way
to be with or without what you love.

They are lined up
like the three of you, mouthpiece to cradle

poised for emergency, or take-off.
And why not,

even on silent mode I can hear their breathing.
I would have been the one to rise to a cough or a snuffle

even when the cots had been moved into quiet rooms of their own.
But there are few rewards to be got

from either too much or too little needing
and these days, with days and hours of distance between us,

I rarely sleep for longer than a few minutes at a time.
I guess what I am trying to say

is that even without lines
or definition, I would not miss your call.

The Visit

Some days

I find him asleep in his chair
head hung as though bashful or ashamed.
Something gentle in his breathing undisturbed
so that to disturb it would be like a cruel wind
come to unsettle the peace of things.
Best to remain unannounced
to rest nestled against his large shoulder.
To lay my worn hand over his, soft as a baby's
and feel how such a deep sleep
smoothes out the wrinkles.

Just at the moment

time began slipping away that was the moment he asked me
Don't you have anyone you can talk to?
I had been holding his hand all day.
Do you want me to go?
Amazing how everything - the tufts in his nose his ears
the hair he has left on his head and beard
has all dissolved into white except for his brow
still red with consternation.
No he says *I don't want you to go.*
It's just that - he looks troubled.
I'm not sure I can help you.

Today

a woman called Sylvia wants to leave.
She is saying this as I arrive and my father
is turning the page of a newspaper.
I can't stay here says Sylvia.
She is wearing her coat and carrying her handbag.
Can someone call me a taxi? –
Sylvia asks for taxis the way my father turns the pages of the paper.

She says her son is expecting her, that he will be here soon.
My father peers through his glasses at the newsprint
while the nurses tell Sylvia she should sit and wait.
The nurses tell Sylvia that her son has telephoned.
I have a son? Sylvia is surprised.
She sits down like they asked her to.
My father raises his head noticing I am here
and looks as if he means to discuss with me
something that he has just read.

Composition

That first morning when the snow
made everything clean like a hospital bed,
I thought of the sheet of paper
your poet friend gave to you
saying, *Write! Write anything.*

All I could see, apart from my own tracks
were those the deer had made.
Turning without purpose,
circling inward
looking for something.

Still

You left your shoes in the hallway,
where I tripped over them
kicking and cursing them as if they were you.
Still left bills unopened saying you knew
what was in them there was no point in looking.
Still answered yes when I asked you
had you remembered to leave the back door locked
and every time I came home late
mostly without you
I would find that you hadn't.
Any stranger could have walked in
and made himself at home.

Now you're gone I can't move your things from the hall
or open the bills
and I leave the door open –
someone could be out there
cold, as you were in the end
in need of a bed.

Conscience

unwinds itself until
that one still moment
when all that is unimportant, unnecessary
falls away leaving one clear thing to be attended to
limbless, without complication
a single slither.

Lifted

Red scarecrow girl/a slip of a thing
this hollow dried out twig of a thing
blackbird eyes darting like a Don't Look Now vision/object of derision
caught her on CCTV/this hint of a thing
shivering skin-and-bone stick of a thing
rattling about in a size ten coat/ten sizes too big for her frame.

This man/this guard/this brick of a thing
this thick-skinned/hard-nosed prick of a thing
sausage pink fingers came right up behind her
grabbed her shoulder like porcelain china
such a fragile delicate chip of a thing.

The room where they took her/a pit of a thing
windowless/nowhere-to-sit of a thing
they poked and they prodded and picked at the girl
said they'd call the police and tell all the world
what a low-down/uncivilised trick of a thing
and she shook.

This creature/this bird/this wishbone-thin little flit of a thing
featherless/fatherless spit of a thing
she blanked all the voices and fingers and pointing
she left them all there with their out-of-nose jointing
and flew from the room through the back of her mind
this practically invisible/wholly derisible
breakable/shakable/bit of a thing.

I Left My Heart

I. Muir Wood

The Park Ranger said there'd be a storm
by the weekend said that's a good thing
the creek will rise up and the Coho will return
to spawn in freshwater. Three years of feasting

on Pacific fruits and they come back to starve
in the red wooded shade of Sequoian giants -
centenarians who measure life slowly in rings -
and watch them return, fry to fingerling.

The fish are jumping. They rinse the salt
from their scales forget the taste of the sea
push upstream to riffle and then lie still
in the same gravel bed of their infancy

each salmon death silver pink
a new beginning.

II. *You must remember this*

You asked me for news. On Tuesday
I cut his nails, they had grown too long.
If I was his mother I would have known
to bite them off feeling gently with my

tongue for sharp edges protecting the
soft pads of his fingertips, shielding them
with my teeth. I use these clippers clumsily
but only once he winced. *A kiss is just a kiss*

and when I was finished, he smiled.
I could never have done that alone, he said.
The fundamental things apply. Once you
watched your dying friend be washed and

shaved for the last time by his youngest brother.
The tenderest act, you said and so it was
with my father's fingernails that will grow again
and keep on growing after everything else has stopped.

III. Opera Café

San Francisco is not my town he said
as though that might explain his confusion
being taken out on city streets where
tail lights flash bright from red to white

wet rain falls gutters rise and conversation
between strangers buzzes like a bulb
that needs replacing. Where would you
call home? I asked him, ordering Russian

cabbage soup thinking Pittsburgh and
knowing that questions are no longer the
thing that can be answered. *The morning fog
may chill the air I don't care.* He had no

appetite for cabbage which in any case was
not like the one he remembered but
when they brought the cake - chocolate with one
candle - eight waiters in white aprons

and cummerbunds sang happy birthday
with operatic grace and I salted the soup with
my crying leaving that part of me there,
washed by rainwater soaked dry by sawdust

still beating
on the floor of Max's Deli.

When I draw my last breath

I will have my three minions around me:

The one holding the mirror
so she can see clearly
when it stops clouding.

The other with pen and paper in hand
so that those of us who aren't poets can stop wondering,
and those of us who are, can share notes on the imagination.

And finally the little one who waits at the foot of my bed,
carrying her purse, ready with the quarter
to make the call.

Beginnings
(for Martha)

When you said to me,
Mummy, you could be born again as a giraffe
because you love them
you also said that you would always
come back as my child,
no matter what, because –

And I understood for the first time
the meaning of reincarnation:
that each new delivery returns us
absolutely to the beginning.
Your infant body curled tight inside mine.
Rivers rising upwards, becoming rain.

Standing Stones

This lack of words between us
is a longstanding stand off.

From wherever we stand it would appear
that one of us has come to smother
and engulf the other.

It is not our language that separates us
nor the smooth of my skin against the rough of yours.
Not even our palates -

though you have always needed more salt than I can stand
and I have liked the pinch of fire on my tongue
the long burn down the gullet and the fist of heat in my belly.

A lover once told me
it is not good for the soul to eat food cold.

But there are times, you will remember,
when only ice will do.

The gods might reason a rift like ours to be the result
of two parallel faults.

The way that night preys upon day for instance
or water maims as it rises over a dry shore

without invitation.

So let me only ask you this,
a question
more than a plea or excitation.

If somewhere some store of words were found
enough, say, to lay as stepping stones upon the ground

or to lever high like the ancients did
standing tall so shadows might fall
across the impasse, this desert of land between us

would we use them to break the silence,
write it?

A Walk in the Park

7am and still dark, especially where the path leads away from the road under the cover of trees and fallen leaves and there is only the occasional dog-walker to interrupt the solitude. In this city, everyone needs to step out of the light for a moment just to breathe and survive. At the bottom of the park four or five police officers in reflective jackets cluster together as if this is the safe thing to do.

It was the first walk we'd taken since the New Year so a few of us were talking, catching up, though trying not to lose sight of the two in front, always ahead of the rest. They stopped when they saw the police. It was raining. One policeman was handing out notices with WITNESS APPEAL printed across the top in red letters. There was no protection, the ink had already started to run. 'If you think of anything,' the policeman said, 'just call the number.'

This early in the year everything is dark, even the open spaces. *He was wearing a dark green blazer with a blue fleece underneath.* 'We should get on,' said one of the walkers at the front. It was too dark to read so I folded the piece of paper and put it in my pocket. *Balding grey hair and a chequered flat cap.*

He Disappeared Into Complete Silence 1947 (Plate 1)
(after the engraving with text by Louise Bourgeois)

Once there was a girl and she loved a man.
They had a date next to the 8th Street station of the 6th Avenue subway.
She had put on her good clothes and a new hat.
Somehow he could not come.
So the purpose of this picture is to show how beautiful she was.
I really mean she was beautiful.

But being in love is not always beautiful –
harder sometimes I think for the girl than the man.
It can take years to return her to the state that she was
before love made her drown and go underground.
Only now new research has come
to show that love is not all it is cracked up to be, but that

information should be kept firmly under your hat.
It is important for most to believe that even painful love is beautiful
and that despite any hurt it might cause it is something that has come
down from God as a gift to women from men.
There are all kinds of posters that will tell you this in the subway,
at least the one that I saw was pretending that this was

true even though the picture was
of a bald man who obviously thought no girl would want him without a hat
to wear, especially in public places like the subway.
Personally I think that a naked head is beautiful
and fitting on a man
who might, without realising it, come

too easily into an open space, unprotected. Come
into a battlefield say. A battlefield that was
meant only for hard men,
hunters, soldiers with helmets
who are in some way beautiful
like those lone men you see on the subway.

Angels I think you call them. Lone subway
rats who are really men come
onto the train to look for beautiful
girls to rescue. There was
once a man who came onto a train for me like that.
A man without a hat, a man

who could only find beauty underground.
A man whose biggest mistake was that he never found a way to come
up to street level to meet the girl who was waiting for him in her best dress
   and hat.

About Mothers, by Daughters

It's like the blind swoop and swerve of bats,
the way they come too close, always or nearly
in your hair or hanging upside down somewhere
just out of reach. Too close, but not quite far enough
away to want to keep in touch. It's like the furl
and reach of a tree fern, the way the fronds extend
like fingers overhead, not so much the wisp of
a parasol, but a dark canopy shadowing everything.

Pianissimo

Where has it gone, his temper, the hot
spit of it?

Here among the *meshuggenas* and
the dribblers

'Let me bring you a napkin,' Shula, the soft brown
Filipino, implores

before his shaking hand spills soup for a
second time

on the shirt the nurse buttoned him into
that morning.

He is changed more times than we were
when we

were in his charge but he knew as little then,
as now,

of what needed doing. The only difference, I'd say,
is gentleness.

One for the Heart

First, I have to tell you, it's yellow
not red like Valentine's day, not even pink
like girl's pyjamas or strawberry Jell-O.
And not - despite whatever you might think
easy to get inside. When they tell you
You only have to open your heart what
they don't say is that they will have to
saw your breastbone in half to do it.

But what I want you to know is this -
that the surgeon could have been a midwife,
he slit the pericardium with only a kiss
of his knife, while his hand held your life,
the full blooded *padoom, padoom* coming back
open-vowelled, full-throated cry with barely a slap.

Senescence

Once we were playing at being old, now we're
nearly there,
admitting conspiratorially

the small ways in which our bodies have started
to rebel
against our minds. In company we are

nods and smiles, tea and friendly conversation.
In private
we pull each other aside, find a corner,

to reveal this blemish or that mark, and run
the other's
fingers over parts of ourselves. Touching

previously reserved for doctors or lovers.
Today you
confess to me that you have hard spots near

your mouth which don't seem to be going. 'Do you
get that too?'
you whisper. And with my hand over my mouth,

like the young girl I was, I breathe out in sighed
relief. 'Yes,'
I lie. Because although the spots do not seem

to be hard upon me yet,
they or some other heralding soon will.

Asylum

I ask you about home
and you tell me
that home is where the river runs,
home is where the dates grow
in bunches
and dry, brown in the sun.
Home is where your father
farms the land and drives his horses.
Home is where you have a father,
or did have.

I ask you where you come from
and you say
I come from here.
Here is where you're from,
no back story,
no foreigner's tale
because only strangers are foreign -
and you are not strange,
you are human
like me.

You ask me
how I spend my days
and my nights
and I tell you that I spend my days thinking
and my nights writing poetry in a dark place
so I can try to imagine
what it might be like
to leave a prison behind in one country
only to arrive in another
the next.
You ask me about home
and I tell you.

Adrift

They brought her the dead drowned body of her husband.
That's not him, she cried.
And in a way, it wasn't.

In the same way the child refuses to recognize the grieving mother
who isn't there
or can't be.

Adrift we cannot determine what is ours;
unpick the tears and threads
or pull away, untied.

Not his face anymore.
Not the arms or hands that carried her.

The homes the tide is bringing back
from the flood
are only there in tiny pieces.

All that washes in now
comes in smooth
as a pebbled stone.

Infinite Space

If you flew around space
close to the speed of light
for about four years
you'd come back to Earth
40,000 years into the future.

Imagine the gift of knowing this
and only today I was supposed
to write a poem on the subject
of infinite space.

But I think of those who won't fly
or can't and never will.
I think of all the multiples
of four years that have gone by
without really ever going anywhere.

And I wonder if the future that awaits
those of us who can pick up
enough speed to finally get there,
will be worth the 39,996 years
we missed out on in the process.

Mrs White

She lived in the white house
with the poplar trees out front
and her name was... or was it just
that we called her the White Lady
and the house was a different colour,
brick red or a shabbier brown?

Either way she scared even the bravest
amongst us. Only the boys had
made it past the gate, up the path
to press the bell and only then
because the rest of us dared them to.

I was still awaiting my initiation,
still too small and much too scaredy-cat
to join them. They said she smelled
like the inside of a walnut shell.
I imagined that, trapped
inside folds of grey papery skin.

I never saw her face, or even
the back of her before she was dead.
My mother made me go to the funeral
where everyone else was wearing black
and only Mrs White in her coffin looked kind .

Right there in the church
I decided it was now or never,
breathed in a lungful of lilacs
and walked up to her, eyes closed.
She couldn't devour me now.

On Seeing a Doe in the Prairie by the Bridge

Out there in the cold you don't expect to see anyone.
Glad if you don't, actually.
Time to be alone, find a stump,
brush the mound of snow off,
sit for a while by the creek that's all froze up
and listen, like the deer do.

You are a stranger here
the birds know that -
calling out to one another in their strange tongue
retreat, retreat, retreat.

And all at once she's there,
chestnut markings like a dark target
framed against the vast white
and so are you.
Afraid to reach for your camera,
in case she thinks it's a gun and runs.
In case this moment doesn't last.

At last she looks.
Sees you looking.
Answers your looking with a stare
and you hook eyes like antlers,
both gripped by what you don't know about the other.

And for that long held moment you are both graceful. Forgiven.

Alice

because I love you and want
to say it clothed in sea lace
I have been walking around
for weeks now with a memo

pad and a Walgreens pencil. I'm
here, you say, by Central Park.
I'm cold, when can you get here?
And I'm thinking, where *do*

those ducks actually go in
winter? And did you know
that when you were born
I wanted to call you Phoebe

like the moon but we called you
bright truth instead. No matter
how still and small I become
I think I will always be craning

something in search of you.
But even here, on the corner of 6th
Avenue, reception is not great.
My voice, you say, keeps breaking

up. My head, it feels, is doing the
same. Outside the subway at 59th
the only colour that scrapes the sky
is grey. This morning you told me

about a man with cancer who
played piano and told stories
while you wrote down what
he said word for word because

he asked you to. You waved your
crooked wand - it was Tom Waits
who said that but it's true, you did
and the tears on my face and the

skates on the pond did spell Alice.
In the Magnolia Bakery we drank
mint tea, Earl Grey and hot chocolate
that was too sweet and not hot

enough. It's because I love you,
you said with a maturity I never
gave you and my mind was
drifting with chuckling rubbish

and pearl weed and it did seem then
that the whole of Manhattan might be
draped in it, sea lace, and that I could
be held in the tangle of its strings.

Wednesday

The bird that used to sing out there, the one we both listened to, the one you said was saying *it could never be like that, it could never be like that, not for me it couldn't* has stopped singing. Have you noticed? There was a different one today in the pear tree which, by the way, is not suffering because of the ivy, it just needs pruning. This one went, *it is this, it is this, look now it is.* But who knows what they mean when they sing?

The spines on these books are all crusty. I'm absolutely certain they can't have been dusted before they were packed. Have you tried opening them? The pages are hard and crack when you turn them. Like dead leaves. How can anything like that be kept for eternity? I don't think we can even give them away.

Recycling is on Tuesday, Thursday and Saturday. If you don't get there by 11 they won't let you in. DEPOSIT ALL UNWANTED ITEMS HERE. They say all but there are strict rules about what should be regarded as unwanted. Your father's things for example. There are categories, standards. It's a dump. You can't just expect them to take everything.

Recipe

Do you remember, maybe you don't, what it was I ordered
and how, when it was brought, the taste of it, the smell,
melted with each mouthful, disappeared and unrecorded,
and I wanted you to ask the waiter before he brought the bill?
It is not, I know, a question of ingredients distilled
or even now the careful reconstruction, bite by bite.
Not the sweet and not the salt of it, how much, how to and when until
but just perhaps to measure the incomprehensibility of night.

Or how an unanticipated morning in October surfaces,
a mother finds her son's cold body stilled in sleep.
How in that moment she must gather all the unmet promises
and all remembering becomes the search for recipe;
to piece together all the moments never tasted of,
to recreate, concoct afresh the elements of love.

Loneliness

      This time you watched me pack,
hoisted yourself
              from the slump of the sofa
as if you were preparing to travel too.
You followed me through ticket barriers
and onto the airplane,
                  squeezing in between
me
    and the couple in the same row
with the child they couldn't stop adoring.
                Did you even have a ticket?

      Exhausted by customs, or maybe a little miffed
because of the conversation
I'd struck up with the gentleman across the aisle
in transit three days
          already from Nigeria
              to see his American grandson,
you trailed a little behind me
when we entered the subway
                with our bags.
And I thought I'd lost you in the heave
of faces but you were there
by my side
        when you saw me corralled
in the corner of the train with the guy
playing
        hip hop on his iPhone, and talking loudly to himself.

      Though your determination wavered a little,
wouldn't you say,
            with that sudden display
of rain
        that hit us on the corner of Atlantic -

a downpour that had even Brooklyn strangers
smiling
          at each other in sympathy.
Or was it just that when I finally remembered
                              to switch on my phone
the memory was already full with unread messages?
For a while I thought you
                    might not stay the course,
but once the skies had cleared and
                         everyone else was back
to their daily business, you found
your feet again
              and anchored in.

      I moved over in the apartment
and made a place for you in bed
hungry
         suddenly, like a lover,
for the sheets to infuse with the smell of you.
This morning we woke in each other's
                              arms,
a half inch of Woodford Reserve
in the toothbrush glass on the table beside me,
crumbs
      on the pillow from rye toast and coffee the night before,
a crumpled bar napkin you must have given me,
and that purple stain on the covers
                    where I'd fallen asleep,
trying
     to write a sonnet
                 in your honour.

Wilson Avenue

He wants to go back to 319 Wilson Avenue
to the porch where his mother sat paring apples
into a bowl, the long peel spiralling
like the smoke from his father's cigar.

He's been having trouble remembering things
but now needs only to connect the pieces
of one small puzzle, a telephone number
to let them know he's coming home.

There are things he might want to forget -
the look on his mother's face when he'd let go
his brother's hand, watched him run to meet
the 1927 Chevy pick-up (best on the street!)

then carried him back, limp in his arms.
Seeing the colour drain from her long red hair
the way it had already drained from her son's
eyelids, closed like the petals of the iris flags

that fluttered at the sides of the house.
*They're dead, Mikey. Mom and Dad are gone.
I don't have a number to give you.* He remembers
the license plate on the truck, PA 59-004,

and the Pittsburgh driver at the funeral
where Mikey wished he'd learned bugle,
not saxophone, so he could have held
his mother with one arm while he played

one-handed with the other. *If you don't give me
the number you're not my sister anymore.*
Fading light dims the sight, no more *Dayenu*,
real Americans now. Taps at the end of the day.

All he wants is to go back. But he should phone
before he goes, to make sure someone is at home.

The Art of Forgetting

Pare away all surfaces
core the middle
lift out by the stem
extract all seeds, scatter them
wait for new shoots to grow
shield them from light
watch them unfurl, translucent
pull gently from the roots
crush to extract all juices
dissolve slowly on your tongue.

On Age and Beauty

If there is to be a perfect age
when beauty comes and finds its home in you
then who could blame the bellowing and rage?
If there is to be a perfect age
when so many may not ever make that stage
reaching out or back when days are few.
If there is to be a perfect age
when beauty comes and finds its home in you.

It is not just a quest to find ourselves
or become ever wiser with the years
we simply have to learn to build more shelves.
It is not just a quest to find ourselves
but rather learn to distance life from health
discover ways to smile through our tears.
It is not just a quest to find ourselves
or become ever wiser with the years.

Though darkness may engulf while love's forgot
your whispers are the hardest sound to hear
why should we wish we were what we are not?
Though darkness may engulf while love's forgot
this day by day revolve we cannot stop
or progress along the road without a mirror.
Though darkness may engulf while love's forgot
your whisper's still the hardest sound to hear.

Blighted

He told me about the one in the bag
that would go bad,
and turn all the others.
He said it as though
he knew something about
potatoes,
as if proximity was the problem.
But I was sure, I said
that there were some with such thick skins,
the red ones perhaps
or those that had been pulled
from the ground so hard
that the tightness of the mud
should have been enough
to squeeze the life out of them
and didn't.
There must be some, I said
that could last a whole autumn
without going soft.
And he looked at me with soft eyes
and pity
because naivety too, he said
is a blight.

Leaving

You came with me to see my father. 'This is your son-in-law,'
I told him. He looked mildly pleased as though having something
in law made the visit all the more significant. The sun was

unusually strong for November and the season's colours were everywhere.
'Let's write a cinquain!' I suggested, thinking we might capture the
scene and that a poem of five lines and twenty-two syllables might

still be within reach if we all worked together. The first line should
be our subject, two syllables long. 'What shall we call this?' I held up
what the vine maple had dropped. 'Leaf,' he said. 'Oh yes,' I said,

'but we need one more syllable.' 'Leaves,' he said, his intelligence
outmatching the form. 'Brown leaf?' I offered. His was better.
The second line is four, it should tell us what it looks like.

He looked at me quizzically. What else was there to describe? 'It's curled,'
you said, 'and dry.' Coming to my rescue just when I was about to fall
headfirst into my father's void. 'Oh yes, curled and dry, and look!

There are veins just like on your hands.' My father stretched out his
fingers and gazed at the underside of his wrist and the back of his hand,
following the trajectory. Dorsal digital veins, blue rivers coursing

Basilic and Cephalic routes. Something flickered, a doctor's curiosity,
and for a moment, that was all the description necessary. Six syllables
for the third line, something to do with purpose. He looked incredulous.

A leaf is just a leaf, surely. Nothing more. I was harrying and he did
not want to be harried. 'An action?' I coaxed. 'It blows in the wind,'
you said and right there, that's why I married you. Swooping in like

Superman to save me. Yes, yes. The wind blows, the leaf falls and
there we have it, six syllables. Two, four, six... and now, eight.
At the sound of counting my father finds renewed interest,

something he'd once been good at. Eight syllables to tell us what
the subject feels like. My father nods his head and breathes out
a sigh that sounds almost like laughing. You suggest 'sad' and I say

'wistful,' and we both think about how we will leave here soon.
The last line is an echo of the first, two syllables. The sun has
changed its position and now we are sitting in almost complete shade.

My father pulls his cap on over his head and you release the brakes
to push the chair on ahead. I wait to write the whole thing down
for him and place it with the leaf in his room where he can see it.

> *brown leaf*
> *such dry curled veins*
> *falls from trees when wind blows*
> *a bit sad, wistful, autumn starts*
> *leaving*

Travel Sickness

Listening to the radio, a child's death,
not your own. Another mother's grief
and suddenly the disembodied nature
of it all has you reaching for the edge
of the seat to steady yourself, the walls
of your mouth too dry to swallow. You
scan old emails, search for the itinerary
she sent before she left, some way to
determine an exact point of location.

Passerine

Stick thin does not convey
what my body meant all those years ago
when no amount of closeness could touch the bone.

Even in that bird like frame
I managed to find some space to hide away in,
though there is not a measuring instrument to locate the centre.

--

Birds do not sing according
to human notions of pitch and time.
Take the White-throated Sparrow for example.

Do not think it calls for
Old Sam Peabody, Peabody, Peabody
or anyone else for that matter. Consider only that it calls.

Consider, too, the *Passer Domesticus*,
which you will know as the House Sparrow.
Normally without a song unless kept too long inside a cage.

Inconspicuous, it lives near to the ground,
and in captivity grips its perch with four strong toes.
Only its hatchlings are helpless.

Bird Box

I woke with the taste of feathers in my mouth,
you should have seen the carnage.
I kept quiet the way a soldier must,
telling myself I'd only meant to protect.

You laughed (so did George) when I showed you how
I'd made a nest in the box
- the one we'd used for sorting Alice's books -
how it opened its beak, looked at me for food like I was its mother.

I used two of our new ramekins - the ones
we bought for making crème brûlée.
I put in water and seeds,
sunflower and pumpkin, one or two blackberries.

It ate the seeds, coloured the water purple
with its excrement. I felt achieved.
In one end, out the other,
as though I could judge what was good for it.

Afterwards I didn't want to tell.
No one had ordered me to do it.
I had volunteered myself,
imagined I really knew how to rescue.

George said I had betrayed the cats
Told me I'd *interrupted the inevitable*.
I kept the lid on, box dark,
though now I can't close my eyes without seeing.

I watched its wing strengthen,
and the shit turn mustard yellow, like a baby's.
Imprisonment at night didn't feel so bad.
Days were harder, without sun.

I let it *go across enemy lines*. I should have known.
The bird perched on my finger
sat for a moment before hopping down
onto the grass, under bushes.

The cats were only doing their job
and I'd messed up mine big time.
What mother doesn't know who
to look out for, or when it's safe to let go?

There were feathers everywhere.
I had cream and sugar on my porridge
this morning. Won't tell that either.
Even without feathers it was... how to say

recognisable. How do they manage that?
To regurgitate it whole, head and body intact?
There was once a time,
when I could do that too.

I prowled, hunted at night, ate furiously.
I could bring things back up again whole.
Only the crumbs, like these feathers
left a clue. I felt like God briefly, back then.

We all hope for rescue. Like you, home late
suggesting we sit together, watch TV.
Tired because we keep missing each other.
I said something catty, you said something died

inside. I felt like God, a little, and cried.

Victory

'Kerpow!' he said, 'blew that one clean out of the water,'
and fish weren't the only thing on his mind.
Napalm and mustard gas, mutilating the enemy
and leaving loved ones far behind.
These things too, took up the hours.
Ah, and that isn't the only way
we measure success these days;
casting out the line, angling the distance
between determination and kindness.

Perhaps the most disturbing
thing of all though is the way I have
begun to regard the fluctuating happiness of friends
as a barometer, an indication of the time
we have left to enjoy ourselves. Fortunately
I've come to realise that not all good things
are necessarily the things that we want
and not all that we want is likely to be either kind or good.

There is a new science, the science of emotions.
It's in a book my daughter showed me.
The theory claims a place for feelings
in the recounting of history.
Not just the body count in wars then,
but the number of tears wept too.

'Yessir!' the man whooped, his fist punching the air.
He must have been pleased about something,
perhaps the fish he'd caught or something else -
an act of bravery or kindness. Victory.
It's still the word to remember on History tests.
Still the song to sing on marches.
Still the way your voice sounds against mine
when you struggle to bring me out of the shadows.
Bugle your high notes in the morning,
always that little bit too sharp.

Impossible Beauty

Oh my god
impossible beauty
diamond cuts searing
razor sharp scars
mutilating edges
of tiny white cells
with scarlet crusts
on stretched skin
a child's moon face
suckling night.

I was there to tell stories

in between the spaces of theirs
that wouldn't be told.
I gathered them in like threads
weaving strands of their eyes, faces
tiny feet in furry slippers
Spiderman pyjamas and a small pair
of butterfly wings.
What is your name?
I asked her.
She might have been the princess in my story
thin yellow hair wisped across
white moon head.
She smiled shyly
despite the tubes in her nose
and the raw plastic barely covering
that place on her wrist.
The back of her hand
impossibly pale
like pure flax spun so fine
you might even think
that she, like the emperor
had nothing covered at all.
She didn't tell me her name.
Why should she?
I was only there to tell stories
pupa to moth in one day,
then gone.

Later when I drove away,
my car squeezed into traffic
no ambulance could have flashed through.
All the way home
my thoughts ran blood-thick
empty of stories.
My head a tight cocoon.

Sorting the Album

When he looked at the image on the front
he was reading information from the back of the one before.
The picture opposite the caption *Me and you eating ice-cream*
was actually Golden Gate Bridge deserted
with the October sun setting behind it,
and the one that read *Martha, your granddaughter*
was in fact my father as a young man.

Getting the captions right is no problem,
an afternoon's work perhaps
writing the words out again on scraps of paper
and slipping the right story into the plastic sleeve...

The real question is how to choose in the first place
what pictures to include - make sense of a life.

driving with alice

through alexandra palace
we see a man with two women
one woman is being held by the others
the man is shaking her
he has his hands round her neck
oh my god I say
and alice says yes
and she drives slowly
close to the edge
he's killing her I say
and alice says yes I know
the man leans in
kicks the woman
who is already puffed and bruised
and in a way
already dead
then he is moaning
maybe even beginning to mourn her
he presses his fingers
into her eyes
as if he is closing them for the last time
this time with love
with longing
maybe even remorse
for what he has done
and in the car we are
what's the word
winded
by what we have seen

The thing is I know it is dangerous
to let my daughter drive
with such distraction.
I should have taken the wheel
and now I can't sleep.
I did nothing, I say, but no one hears it.

I couldn't save her.
My sheets are wet with sweat.
Nothing, I say again,
shouting into the pillow
to smother the noise.

After Making Love on a Sunday Morning

I smelt my Grandma's house
in the sweat of my armpits.
You joked that you knew where to go then
when you needed that sensation.
But there in the half light
Sunday morning nearly gone
I was remembering
all that is unrecoverable.

Fruit

When he was a boy his mother let him crack open a watermelon with his father's hammer. The red flesh went everywhere. For years afterwards they still found dried pulp, spray of splattered juice on the wall next to the patio, and a few black seeds stuck between the paving stones. When he grew up, he thought, he would fix all that. No one wants the mess inside to explode over everything, and stay there. There has to be a cleaner way.

Moving the Stag Head to Aunt Irma's

The same day they
signed the divorce papers
a tornado hit the house.
I'll be damned, she said,
there goes our security.

Last September they had
to move the bed into
the dining room because
their folks couldn't use
the stairs anymore.

For fourteen years
they slept skin to skin.
This is the first pair
of pyjamas I have ever
owned, she told him.

He backed the U-Haul
into the garage to load
his graduation pictures
and the stag head
she never liked anyway.

Afterwards he never saw
the girls. She got a new
boyfriend and a red dress
which was the wrong
size so she took it back.

He moved in with his
mother's sister and she
moved the white painting
ladder from the front to the
back of the house.

She left the couch outside
on the porch when she took
the kids to live with her
half the time in Steve's trailer
with no air conditioning.

The guy at the store said
the weather's looking bad
again this year but she said
the insurance will cover it
now the State's got custody.

Ices

Once I told my therapist about a dream I had.
It was hot, there were two of us, we saw a sign
that said ICES. I told her Ices but my therapist
thought I said Isis. She's Greek, my therapist.

Isis was a goddess in Ancient Egyptian religious
beliefs, worshipped throughout the Greco-Roman
world. You can see why my therapist might have
wanted to think I said Isis, not Ices. The sign said

Ices, I was sure of it. Like popsicles, frozen drinks
on a stick. Sugary, sticky and sweet. The goddess
Isis, my therapist told me, was the first daughter
of Geb, god of the earth, and Nut, goddess of the

overarching sky. I did not want to disappoint my
therapist but I did not dream of the goddess Isis
who, my therapist said, was the friend of slaves,
sinners and artisans. Goddess of motherhood, magic

and fertility who gathered the parts of her beloved
dead husband and restored his body back to life.
It was hot and there were two of us. In my dream
perhaps I was thinking an ice lolly might be the thing

to cool us both down. A treat. I did not think more
about the significance of ice. The Ancient Egyptians,
maybe the Greeks too, believed the Nile flooded every
year with her tears. I dreamt of ice, not Isis, I told her.

Word Birth

I'm trying to remember another time
when a poem would wake me
in the middle of the night
splish splat
with its need to be written.

Not the spit hit of wind on the window pane
like a midnight battalion
firing bullets of rain
slash sleet
that massacre sleep.

Not the next to me closeness, the blanket spread
the snore shore of breathing
breaking waves in the bed
slide stretch
sluicing into my dreams.

Not the snuffle of fear like a burglar's creep
the creak crack on the stair
or the tread of some feet
sneak slip
breaking into the night.

Just the quiet moment a thought unannounced
breezes in like a draught
moves itself right round until
shhhhh
it's born onto the page.

Scientific Autobiography

'An experiment is a question which science poses to Nature, and a measurement is the recording of Nature's answer.'
   - Max Planck, *A Scientific Autobiography and Other Papers, 1949*

First there is the hypothesis:
if I am not that then I must be this.
But how are we to come to a conclusion?
The determinist says one thing, the indeterminist another.
Each wants to be right in their solipsistic fashion.
Take these body particles for example,
could they have come from anyone else?
What the subject does and doesn't know
is that the very word 'real' is only relative
and among all the proven facts we have available,
there is only one that is absolutely the most certain.
And since exact science depends on logic and measurability,
I am an experiment that cannot be undertaken.

Wait To Be Called

I have been holding on and you are busy letting go, damn you. Ignoring the way that patch of sunlight this afternoon has wrapped itself like a bandage around the whole trunk of the tree you said was leaning so far over itself the roots won't hold until Fall. This time next year our children will have forgotten everything we told them and isn't that the whole point about making a will, that a thought's not worth a doughnut unless it's written down?

I haven't chosen to be by myself but it would seem that loneliness makes its own choices about who it spends time with. The books on my side of the bed are still in colour, while yours have faded almost entirely into monochrome. We can't even compare notes anymore. Where does that leave shared vision?

Or Not to Be

You were once the prince
of Denmark after all
and madness reigned
in that household
so it shouldn't have surprised me
when even after telling you
for the third time in one sitting
that I am not one of the nurses
or even a doctor like you
but your daughter,
middle one of three,
you didn't seem that interested
or bothered, or concerned.
Perhaps you just didn't know
that such a thing
might have mattered once.
But even you were astounded
at the nobility of your own mind when,
there we were, all hubble and bubble
struggling to recall those few famous lines
given to one who felt himself to be drowning
in an altogether different sea of troubles
and it was you who remembered
word-perfect, the question
and all the slings and arrows that followed.
So magnificent yes, and outrageous perhaps
that this is the way we will finally end our struggle
without arms or opposition.

Schizophrenic

Now I lie awake in the bed he was born in,
a prison to match his, locked here until morning.
Is there no consolation, no balm for the mind?
I despise those empty words, *Cruel to be kind.*

He is my son, I should be showing off his trophies
or nursing, milky-eyed, these letters that he wrote me.
Clozapine... Olanzapine... Quotiapine...
Mummy, Mummy, where have you been? I've been to London to –

Let Her Majesty's services take him now,
at forty a boy must leave home somehow.
And soon soon his voices will smooth out his pain
while mine will replay again and again and again and again

the voice on the telephone when I'd dialled three nines
Ambulance? Fire? No, police... please, this time.

The Starlet

Big fame? she said, equals a small death.

They've already had all of you while you were alive. Nothing to pick over after you've gone.

Oh I've seen them, those tiny bits of broken star shooting across the universe for a tiny second and then nothing. Not even time to make a wish.

Promising? Stay that way. Keep 'em waiting. Give them something to stew over after you've really gone.

If only, they'll say. *She might have been something...*

Let them wallow. It's the *might have* that makes us great.

Done

Tonight I want to be read aloud to in bed.
I'm done with eyes and deciphering lines.
Done with looking too close,
that seeing thing.
Finished with the grip of the pen
or even being the teller of stories.
Leave that to others now -
tonight I will savour only your voice;
paperless, weightless
without permanence.

Maternal Encounters and Thoughts Arising

I have been reading a book about mothers
their distinct and indistinct qualities
how they are defined by interruptions,

and I want to say something too –
that I am one that I have one
and that I long for something different

something other and perhaps this is the point
to interrupt the name itself; a name I wasn't
born with but born to and through birthing

became one myself. And maybe this is it,
that it is in the interrogation of the name
that otherness finally reveals itself –

the way the other hides behind undulating waves
under rumpled cover, the two-humped blanket of M,
how she the mother baring her breasts, bra-less

and unprotected, invites the hiss and slither
of snakes and then turns to smother. In this one
act we are all the same; daughters, lovers, sons,

desiring only separateness, lack of interruption
to be once more apart, disconnected, alone – I.
And my evidence is this; suspended in dark space,

just above or just below the mother's embrace
the child squirms and wriggles slipping out of reach,
and the prickly-spined teen grows ever more cactus-like

demonstrating that closeness will lead
eventually to distance,
and that every kiss is also a sting.

Correspondence with the Care Home

It's important you be put in the picture
I wanted to show you this photograph;
now that he is entering the final stages.
my father delicately holding a buttercup.
He does not brighten like he used to at visits,
He can no longer communicate but he held
the medication is no longer benefitting him.
this flower and was looking at it so intently
Choosing resuscitation could be futile as he
I could sense he'd been touched by its beauty.
would not return to life in a meaningful way.

Snapshot

The girl is smiling, it is not a lie.
She is squeezing her lips together,
using them to cover her teeth which are too spread out in her mouth.
There are too many gaps,
enough for you to put your tongue straight through.

She is hiding something on her bottom lip –
a birthmark. She doesn't mind but others seem to.
It will be off in a few year's time,
a quick slice of the surgeon's knife
and you won't see it again.

She is waiting for the flash,
determined not to blink this time.
She wants you to remember seeing her just like this,
with her eyes open.